Understanding Dreams

HEALS THE SOUL

Dream and Vision Interpretation
in Healing Prayer

Understanding Dreams

HEALS THE SOUL

Dream and Vision Interpretation
in Healing Prayer

Dale Shannon

UNDERSTANDING DREAMS HEALS THE SOUL
DREAM AND VISION INTERPRETATION IN HEALING PRAYER

To contact the author about speaking at your conference or church, please go to:

Fulfill Your Dream
Manhattan Beach, CA 90266
www.fulfillyourdream.org

OTHER BOOKS BY DALE SHANNON:
Fulfill Your Dream and Destiny
Life Purpose Coaching
How to Be an Overcomer

Scripture taken from the Holy Bible, NEW INTERNATIONAL VERSION®, NIV® Copyright © 1973, 1978, 1984, 2011 by Biblica, Inc.® Used by permission. All rights reserved worldwide.

Scripture quotations taken from the New American Standard Bible® (NASB),
Copyright © 1960, 1962, 1963, 1968, 1971, 1972, 1973,
1975, 1977, 1995 by The Lockman Foundation
Used by permission. www.Lockman.org

Scripture taken from the New King James Version®. Copyright © 1982 by Thomas Nelson.
Used by permission. All rights reserved

Italics in Scripture quotations have been added by the author for emphasis.

Copy Editor, Interior Layout and Formatting: Tammie Pelletier
Cover and Interior Design and Layout: Christian Wetzel

ISBN-13: 978-0578402932
ISBN-10: 0578402939

ENDORSEMENTS

Dale Shannon has put together an amazing tool in this book. There are many materials out there on the subject of dreams, but what I love about Dale's book is that she bridged the gaps in process in a lot of the popular dream training and she was able to bring the practical approach married to the deep Spiritual understanding. She provides a Biblically based model that will help empower you to understand your dreams as parables which will bring great significance and meaning to your life as well as for those around you. I love how she breaks down the categories of dreams and contrasts them to visions and other encounters and then gives us an interpretation model that is so sound that you will use it for the rest of your life. I highly recommend this book and the author to you!

Shawn Bolz
Author of Translating God, Modern Prophets, and God Secrets
www.bolzministries.com

Dale Shannon has an amazing dream life and a profound gift to interpret and apply dreams for people, groups and even nations. Over the years we have known her as not only a prolific intercessor but also possessing a unique ability to teach people how to apply their dreams to their lives and bring them to freedom and fullness in their destiny. Her husband Doug and Dale are great friends and I am sure you will not only be blessed - but changed - when you read her amazing biblical insights and personal revelation regarding dreams as well as an understanding of the heavenly courts.

Bon Appetit!

Charlie Robinson
Revival Canada Ministries

Dale Shannon has had a great influence on me, helping to lay a foundational understanding of dreams and dream interpretation in my life. She taught me practically as she interpreted many of my dreams. You will find the well-written Understanding Dreams Heals the Soul a valuable addition to your library.

Paul L. Cox
Aslan's Place, Apple Valley, CA.

Dale brings a passion of helping people become more intimate with the Lord. This manual has both a personal and yet thorough understanding of how to respond and steward dreams. You will receive a breakthrough in your life in this specific area. Having traveled internationally with Dale, I have witnessed her accuracy and hunger in the area of the prophetic. She lives what she teaches and this is born of her genuine journey.

Mark Tubbs
HIM Missions Apostle
Founder of Transformation of the Nations

TABLE OF CONTENTS

ACKNOWLEDGMENTS

I thank my husband, Doug Shannon, for his love, encouragement, and support in writing this book.

I thank all my leaders and mentors who saw something good in me and called it out. You know who you are, and I appreciate every encouraging word. I especially thank John Paul Jackson, and Barbie Breathitt for mentoring me and imparting dream interpretation skills and stretching me through much practice to develop the skill. I thank Shawn Bolz, Dr. Paul Cox, and Joe Gil for encouragement and opening doors of opportunity to teach and impart dream interpretation through their ministries. I thank Charlie Robinson for revelatory insight, encouragement and friendship. Thank you for stretching me to grow.

I want to thank the thousands of students from around the world that I've taught various "Dream Understanding Heals the Soul", and "Fulfill Your Dream and Destiny" seminars. Additionally, I thank the hundreds of clients I've had the privilege of ministering to personally and hearing your heart. Through each of you, the Lord has taught me much about dream understanding, healing of the soul, renewing the mind, and living the ascended life. I bless you all.

I want to thank the prophetic and dream teams I have led throughout the years. I thank each you for teaching me through your dreams and visions. You are awesome and I believe in you.

INTRODUCTION

Is God speaking to you today in your dreams? Understanding dreams can be a key to rapid healing of the soul for you and others. By understanding your dreams, using Biblically based methods, your intimacy with God will increase as you discover how God is speaking to you, so that you can be aligned to His love and purposes. This unique teaching emphasizes how you can live victoriously by taking authority in your dreams over hindrances and conflicted soul areas resulting in wholeness of the soul. This teaching empowers you to understand God's picture language, and to be aware of the enemy's plans and possible traps that could cause you to be stuck. Restoration and healing results as you take authority in your dreams or visions, and a deeper intimacy develops with your father God.

Chapter 1

IMPORTANCE OF
DREAMS

God has always desired to communicate with us, His people, because He loves us. He is not a silent, distant, indifferent Creator who rules the universe having little interest in the lives of His children. Not only does God want to speak to His people, but also He is concerned with the smallest details of our lives. Throughout Scripture we see a God who cares and who communicates His concerns, His direction, His judgments and His blessings to the people of this world.

In the ancient Near East, in the Babylonian, Egyptian, Greek, and Roman cultures, dreams were understood to be communication from a deity. This included the Hebrews who believed that the one true God (Yahweh) spoke to His people in dreams. Kings and priests could change the direction of a society based upon a dream. Rulers often included in their royal courts those who sought and interpreted dreams. We see examples of this with Daniel and Joseph.

The Old Testament contains accounts of dreams and visions received by Israelites *(Solomon in 1 Kings 3 and Abraham in Genesis 15)* and non-Israelites *(Abimelech in Genesis 20 and Nebuchadnezzar in Daniel 4)*.

Ancient people valued dreams as communication from God. God has always spoken to mankind through the realm of the Spirit in dreams. God is spirit and speaks to our spirits giving us His divine plan. He's already written out what we'll do in our lives and He gives us dreams so we'll know step by step how to fulfill our destiny and calling.

God has a divine dream plan that enables us to reach our destiny in Him. God's Holy Spirit, the Spirit of Truth will lead us into all truth. He'll reveal things about us. When we're asleep we don't argue with God or give excuses; we agree with Him. The Holy Spirit hovers over us in the night season and impregnates us, His people with dreams that keep us searching for what they mean.

God has always desired to communicate with us, His people, because He loves us. He is not a silent, distant, indifferent Creator who rules the universe having little interest in the lives of His children. Not only does God want to speak to His people, but also He is concerned with the smallest details of our lives. Throughout Scripture we see a God who cares and who communicates His concerns, His direction, His judgments and His blessings to the people of this world.

In the ancient Near East, in the Babylonian, Egyptian, Greek, and Roman cultures, dreams were understood to be communication from a deity. This included the Hebrews who believed that the one true God (Yahweh) spoke to His people in dreams. Kings and priests could change the direction of a society based upon a dream. Rulers often included in their royal courts those who sought and interpreted dreams. We see examples of this with Daniel and Joseph.

The Old Testament contains accounts of dreams and visions received by Israelites *(Solomon in 1 Kings 3 and Abraham in Genesis 15)* and non-Israelites *(Abimelech in Genesis 20 and Nebuchadnezzar in Daniel 4)*.

Ancient people valued dreams as communication from God. God has always spoken to mankind through the realm of the Spirit in dreams. God is spirit and speaks to our spirits giving us His divine plan. He's already written out what we'll do in our lives and He gives us dreams so we'll know step by step how to fulfill our destiny and calling.

God has a divine dream plan that enables us to reach our destiny in Him. God's Holy Spirit, the Spirit of Truth will lead us into all truth. He'll reveal things about us. When we're asleep we don't argue with God or give excuses; we agree with Him. The Holy Spirit hovers over us in the night season and impregnates us, His people with dreams that keep us searching for what they mean.

Our spirit man cries out for spirit. As Christians, our spirit connects with the Holy Spirit, but when people's spirit is searching, they may go to counterfeit spirits of truth, the psychics, and the false to find answers. Dream interpretation comes from God and only those that know God intimately can give an interpretation of a spirit dream.

As Christians, we need to study to show ourselves approved and to be able to offer truth to those that are searching. God's end-time revival comes through the outpouring of His Holy Spirit upon all flesh, the saved and the unsaved. God's given to us keys to bring those in darkness into the light. The prophets of old looked to our time. He saved the best for last.

> *And it shall be in the last days, God says, that I will pour forth of my Spirit upon all mankind; and your sons and your daughters shall prophesy, and your young men shall see visions, and your old men shall dream dreams; even upon My bond slaves, both men and women, I will in those days pour forth of My Spirit, and they shall prophesy.*

And I will grant wonders in the sky above, and signs on the earth below, blood, and fire, and vapor of smoke. The sun will be turned into darkness, and the moon into blood, before the great and glorious day of the Lord shall come. And it shall be that everyone who calls on the name of the Lord will be saved.
Acts 2:17–21 (NASB)

In this passage, upon whom is God pouring out His Spirit?

God is pouring out His Spirit on all flesh, wooing everyone to Himself. It is not just Christians or believers who are having spirit dreams, but everyone.

Notice the pronoun change in verses 17 and 18 from your sons, your daughters, your young men, your old men to My bond slaves, both men and women.

What's the significance in the pronoun change?

There's a divine transfer of ownership taking place from your daughters and sons to my men and maidservants. The personal pronoun My emphasizes intimacy and relationship. These individuals are His and hear the Lord more clearly.

Notice also the distinction between young men seeing visions and the old men dreaming dreams. What's that about? It's about the maturity levels, not age levels. The depth of our understanding comes through spending time with God, reading His Word, and allowing the Holy Spirit to transform us into His image. The Holy Spirit will mature our spirit as we submit to Him.

Although visions are considered a higher level of revelation, they are usually literal making them easier to understand than dreams. The old men and women are those with more maturity who will understand God's communication through dreams. Maturity is needed because dreams are metaphorical and not easily understood. In dreams one has to interpret symbolism, metaphors, riddles, enigmas, mysteries, puns and riddles. We need to interpret His language.

In these last days, when the Holy Spirit moves, there is and will be an increase in prophecy, dreams, visions, signs and wonders. The result will be a great harvest. We want to operate in the Spirit of Revelation and Understanding, so we will be fruitful in this end time harvest.

Dreams are clearly stated to be one of the means God uses to communicate even though mankind doesn't comprehend the meaning or rationale. If we value our dreams, and pay attention to them, God will speak more to us in the night season. If we study skills in interpreting dreams God's way and rely on the Holy Spirit, we will be the ones to help others understand how God is speaking to them through their dreams.

Chapter 2

GOD SPEAKS IN
DREAMS & PARABLES

Dreams come in God's picture language. The book of Revelation is in pictures. We must learn God's dream language. He speaks to us through a language of pictures, symbols, types and shadows. Our minds are picture oriented and we can remember the pictures easier than remembering words. In the spirit realm, communication is thought by thought. There is no time or distance in the Spirit realm. The spirit realm is not confined to time as we are in the natural.

The Holy Spirit can cause you to transcend time and space barriers of the past, present and future in our dreams. If God takes you back in time, it may be to be healed of what happened in the past, or if He takes you to the future, it's to show you the great exploits you will do. God loves to reveal to His people the future, and often He seals it, until our character is big enough to handle it.

> *In a dream, in a vision of the night, when deep sleep falls upon men, while slumbering on their beds, then He opens the ears of men, and seals their instruction. In order to turn man from his deed, and conceal pride from man, he keeps back his soul from the Pit, and his life from perishing by the sword.*
> ***Job 33:15–18 (NKJV)***

God will speak through a dream and a vision. He'll give you a dream and conceal it away and you don't know you have it. Calling dreams can be sealed dreams because you're going to move in the supernatural. God prepares you to walk in your destiny. He comes, plants seed into your spirit, but you don't remember.

These dreams are sealed until an appointed time, and then you do it. He'll seal these dreams to protect you from yourself and pride. It keeps you from becoming prideful.

Surely the Lord God does nothing, unless He reveals His secret to His servants the prophets.
Amos 3:7 (NKJV)

"Hear now My words: If there is a prophet among you, I, the Lord, shall make Myself known to him in a vision. I shall speak with him in a dream."
Num. 12:6 (NASB)

DREAMS ARE NIGHT PARABLES

And the disciples came and said to Him, "Why do you speak to them in parables?" Jesus answered them, "To you it has been granted to know the mysteries of the kingdom of heaven, but to them it has not been granted. For whoever has, to him more shall be given, and he will have an abundance; but whoever does not have, even what he has shall be taken away from him. Therefore I speak to them in parables; because while seeing they do not see, and while hearing they do not hear, nor do they understand. In their case the prophecy of Isaiah is being fulfilled, which says,

'YOU WILL KEEP ON HEARING, BUT WILL NOT UNDERSTAND; YOU WILL KEEP ON SEEING, BUT WILL NOT PERCEIVE; FOR THE HEART OF THIS PEOPLE HAS BECOME DULL, WITH THEIR EARS THEY SCARCELY HEAR, AND THEY HAVE CLOSED THEIR EYES, OTHERWISE THEY SHOULD SEE WITH THEIR EYES, HEAR WITH THEIR EARS, AND UNDERSTAND WITH THEIR HEART AND RETURN AND I WOULD HEAL THEM.'

But blessed are your eyes, because they see, and your ears, because they hear.
Matt. 13:10-16 (NASB)

Revelation, the knowledge of the secrets of the kingdom and eyes to see and ears to hear, is given to those who value it.

Whoever has more will be given.

Jesus said, "You must have eyes to see and ears to hear." Develop your spiritual eyes. "You must understand parables." If you don't, you'll develop a hard heart. Dreams are night parables.

If you cross over to being able to think, and understand parables, grasp the knowledge of the kingdom, you will be given more. If you don't value these things, even what you have, will be taken away. This is the condition of the church today. What they had has been taken away because they haven't valued understanding dreams, and parables. We need to think in both the natural and in the spiritual.

The condition of many Christians today is that they don't understand dreams and have lost discernment. God has chosen to conceal things from those that don't value it and reveal things to those that do.

The concealment of truth is actually the mercy of God to lessen the judgment for a hard-hearted person.

> *In their case the prophecy of Isaiah is being fulfilled, which says,*
>
> *'YOU WILL KEEP ON HEARING, BUT WILL NOT UNDERSTAND; YOU WILL KEEP ON SEEING, BUT WILL NOT PERCEIVE; FOR THE HEART OF THIS PEOPLE HAS BECOME DULL, WITH THEIR EARS THEY SCARCELY HEAR, AND THEY HAVE CLOSED THEIR EYES, OTHERWISE THEY SHOULD SEE WITH THEIR EYES, HEAR WITH THEIR EARS, AND UNDERSTAND WITH THEIR HEART AND RETURN AND I WOULD HEAL THEM.'*
> **Matt. 13:14-16 (NASB)**

We have to get out of the hardness of heart condition (calloused and dull). We need to begin to understand the parables and dreams of the Bible, value our dreams, and ask God to speak to us.

> *"Father, I repent and renounce for myself and my generational line for hardness of heart and for coming into agreement with the doctrine of cessationism, believing that You Lord do not still speak to Your children today, or want a personal relationship with me.*
>
> *Father, will You break off of me the consequences of not believing that the gifts of the Holy Spirit are for today?*
>
> *Lord I choose to receive all that You have for me and I ask for You to speak to me through dreams, visions, and prophetic words. I desire to know what is on Your heart, Father God, so that I can be about Your business.*
>
> *Father, release to me Your dreams and the Spirit of wisdom and revelation."*

> *It is the glory of God to conceal a matter, But the glory of kings to search out a matter.*
> **Prov. 25:2 (NASB)**

It's the glory of a king to search out what God is saying and speaking. You, as a child of God, have been given the privilege by God to go into the King's palace, to go into His storehouse. He wants to give you the keys of revelation to be able to search something out. Being able to understand revelation is about knowing your identity as a son or a daughter of the king. It's about relationship and knowing that in Christ you are royalty in the kingdom of God. As you seek understanding, you will find understanding. In kingship, you can search out the understanding of the revelation He has given to you.

God speaks in a language of signs, symbols, dark sayings, puns, riddles, and mysteries through dreams and visions. We need to be able to interpret His language. Why does God choose to speak to us this way? So we will seek Him. It's a lover's game. It's a lover wooing His bride to draw near and dig deeper. He wants us to go after the revelation. We seek Him out. It causes us to love Him more and to depend upon Him.

God often speaks to me in puns. In one dream I had several years ago, I arrived at the college where I was to teach a summer English class. I was told that the class I was assigned to teach had been given to someone else that had been hired yesterday. This was totally unjust, and in the dream I was not happy at what had happened. "You gave my class to someone who was hired yesterday?" I exclaimed. Then, I was offered another class to teach if I wanted it. I asked, what it was, and the answer was, "Vision. It's yours if you want it." In the dream I thought vision was about the science of eyes - optometry, and since science was not my major, I again was not happy. I woke myself up by saying, "Vision! What do I know about vision?"

 As I woke up, I realized that there are different meanings to the word vision and calmed down. This dream was a calling dream for me to teach on dreams and visions. Dreams can have layers of interpretation. When I was later in Malawi, Africa, and praying for a woman with white glaucoma on her eyes, I asked the Lord to give her vision. As I did, I remembered the dream, and faith rose. The Lord healed her and gave her new vision. The white left her eyes. The natural speaks of the supernatural.

So, God chooses to speak in a concealed way. It requires the Holy Spirit to understand how He speaks. God wants you to search out the matter. Dreams will bypass the resistance of your soul- mind, will and emotions. Dreams may be different from your opinion, training or theology. Dreams may seem too difficult to believe or to fulfill.

God will speak through a dream and a vision. He'll give you a dream and conceal it away and you don't know you have it. Calling dreams can be sealed dreams because you're going to move in the supernatural. God prepares you to walk in your destiny. He comes, plants seed into your spirit, but you don't remember. These dreams are sealed until an appointed time, and then you do it. He'll seal these dreams to protect you from yourself and pride. It keeps you from becoming prideful.

"Indeed God speaks once, or twice, yet no one notices it. "In a dream, a vision of the night, when sound sleep falls on men, while they slumber in their beds, then He opens the ears of men, and seals their instruction, that He may turn man aside from his conduct, and keep man from pride; He keeps back his soul from the pit, and his life from passing over into Sheol."

Job 33:14-18 (NASB)

Dreams can be a preferred method of correction by the Lord. In humility, go over the dream. Sometimes generational issues are revealed and sometimes, sin issues that you weren't aware of are revealed. During the day, sometimes our minds can be are so preoccupied, that it is difficult to hear God. Therefore the Lord will use the night season to speak to you and reveal hidden issues, so that you can deal with them and be set free.

Dreams can be a preferred method of revelation. Dreams are concealed and you'll get less resistance or warfare. There is a factor of clarity verses cost. The greater the clarity of revelation, the greater the cost will be for it to come to pass. If revelation is very clear, you'll get more resistance, and warfare. If God gives you a clear word, it could be because you are or will be going through a testing time of the word. The Lord said to Aaron and Miriam:

He said, "Hear now My words: If there is a prophet among you, I, the Lord, shall make myself known to him in a vision. I shall speak with him in a dream. "Not so with my servant Moses, He is faithful in all My household; with him, I speak mouth to mouth, even openly, and not in dark sayings, and he beholds the form of the Lord. Why then were you not afraid to speak against My servant, against Moses?"

Num. 12:6-8 (NASB)

God will make Himself known in a vision; He'll speak to you in dreams.

There's also face to face communication, and there is dark speech and riddles that God chooses to speak in that way. I want to know Him like Moses, to follow His heart. God will use the dark sayings to draw us closer to Him. We need to seek them out.

Chapter 3
DREAMS
IN THE BIBLE

Dreams and visions are perhaps the most common ways God has communicated with man. Over one third of the Bible relates to dreams and visions and there are more than 50 references to dreams and visions in which God delivered messages.

1. The first dream recorded in scripture was Abraham's dream when God made a covenant with him and his descendants.

    God said to Abram, "Know for certain that your descendants will be strangers in a land that is not theirs, where they will be enslaved and oppressed 400 years.
    Gen. 15:13 (NASB)

2. God warned ungodly kings and rulers through dreams such as Abimelech, a self-condition dream.

    But God came to Abimelech in a dream by night, and said to him, "Indeed you are a dead man because of the woman whom you have taken, for she is a man's wife."
    Gen. 20:3 (NKJV)

    And God said to him in a dream, "Yes I know that you did this in the integrity of your heart. For I also withheld you from sinning against Me; therefore I did not let you touch her."
    Gen. 20:6 (NKJV)

3. Through dreams, Jacob received God's promises regarding his heritage. There is power in vision. What we set before our eyes has an impact on what and who we become. Jacob was given divine instructions in a dream outlining how he was to get wealth from his flock.

And it came about at the time when the flock were mating that I lifted up my eyes and saw in a dream, and behold, the male goats which were mating were striped, speckled, and mottled.

Gen. 31:10 (NASB)

4. God revealed Joseph's destiny through his dreams. In Genesis 37, Joseph had two dreams, which showed his eventual rule over his brothers. God establishes things through a witness of two. Joseph had the dreams when he was 17 and was 30 years old when the dreams finally came true. There were many dreams and interpretations of dreams that brought him from the pit to prison, and finally to the palace as second ruler in Egypt.

He said to them, "Please listen to this dream which I have had; for behold, we were binding sheaves in the field, and lo, my sheaf rose up and also stood erect; and behold, your sheaves gathered around and bowed down to my sheaf."

Now he had still another dream, and related it to his brothers, and said, "Lo, I have had still another dream, and behold, the sun and the moon and eleven stars were bowing down to me."

Gen. 37:6, 9 (NASB)

5. Pharaoh, an ungodly ruler had two dreams.

Then it came to pass, at the end of two years, that Pharaoh had a dream and behold, he stood by the river. Suddenly there came up out of the river seven cows, fine looking and fat; and they fed in the meadow. Then behold, seven other cows came up after them out of the river, ugly and gaunt, and stood by the other cows on the bank of the river. And the ugly and gaunt cows ate up the seven fine looking and fat cows. So Pharaoh awoke. He slept and  *dreamed a second time, and suddenly seven heads of grain came up on one stalk, plump and good. Then behold, seven thin heads, blighted by the east wind, sprang up after them. And the seven thin heads devoured the seven plump and full heads. So Pharaoh awoke, and indeed it was a dream.*

Gen. 41:1-7 (NKJV)

The butler of Pharaoh finally remembered Joseph after he interpreted the butler and the baker's dreams correctly two years earlier.

Pharaoh sends for Joseph, he's taken out of the dungeon, shaved and given new clothing and brought to Pharaoh.

And Pharaoh said to Joseph, "I have had a dream, and there is no one who can interpret it. But I have heard it said of you that you can understand a dream, to interpret it." So Joseph answered Pharaoh, saying, "It is not in me; God will give Pharaoh an answer of peace."

Gen. 41:15-16 (NKJV)

Joseph gives the interpretation of the dream of 7 years of plenty followed by 7 years of famine.

6. Gideon overcame his fear and inferiority complex and became a mighty warrior and leader through understanding his enemy's dream. This was a dream to bring encouragement and confirmation to Gideon as he was seeking the Lord.

And when Gideon had come, there was a man telling a dream to his companion. He said, "I have a dream: To my surprise, a loaf of barley bread tumbled into the camp of Midian; it came to a tent and struck it so that it fell and overturned, and the tent collapsed." Then his companion answered and said, 'This is nothing else but the sword of Gideon the son of Joash, a man of Israel! Into his hand God has delivered Midian and the whole camp.' And so it was, when Gideon heard the telling of the dream and its interpretation, that he worshiped. He returned to the camp of Israel, and said, "Arise, for the Lord has delivered the camp of Midian into your hand."

Judg. 7:13-15 (NKJV)

Gideon was the son of a farmer, and the loaf of barley which was considered an inferior grain which was used by the poor symbolized Israel, and Gideon's army who appeared to be inferior and smaller in number than the Midianite army. The tent represented the entire Midianite camp or army.

7. Daniel had the gift of being able to interpret dreams. Daniel studied his gift and was a learned man versed in many dimensions of training. He excelled over the foreign occult leaders and was called upon by the kings when no one else had the answers.

The King answered and said to Daniel, whose name was Belteshazzar," Are you able to make known to me the dream which I have seen, and its interpretation?" Daniel answered in the presence of the king, and said, "The secret which the king has demanded, the wise men, the astrologers, the magicians, and the soothsayers cannot declare to the king. But there is a God in heaven who reveals secrets, and He has made known to King Nebuchadnezzar what will be in the latter days. Your dream, and the visions of your head upon your bed were these."

Dan. 2:26-28 (NKJV)

Daniel was able to give King Nebuchadnezzar his dream and the interpretation sparing the lives of the Chaldean wise men.

> *The king answered Daniel, and said "Truly your God is the God of gods, the Lord of kings, and a revealer of secrets, since you could reveal this secret." Then the king promoted Daniel and gave him many great gifts; and he made him ruler over the whole province of Babylon and chief administrator over all the wise men of Babylon.*
> **Dan. 2:47-48 (NKJV)**

Only God can reveal the hidden secret things that are sealed in a dream. This is why we need to study God's method of interpreting dreams, so we can reveal to seekers the true understanding of their spirit given dreams.

8. Joseph, the husband of Mary, was a dreamer. He was given a dream where the angel of the Lord appeared to him instructing him to take Mary, though pregnant as his wife (Matt.1:20-21). Later, after Herod was dead, and angel of the Lord appeared in a dream to Joseph in Egypt saying,

> *Now when Herod was dead, behold, an angel of the Lord appeared in a dream to Joseph in Egypt, saying, "Arise and take the Child and His mother, and go into the land of Israel, for those who sought the Child's life are dead."*
> **Matt. 2:19, 20 (NKJV)**

Ezekiel recorded no dreams, but four visions. The book of Revelation was given to John in visionary form. One third of the Bible speaks of dreams and visions, yet much of the church claims that this is not how God speaks today.

Dreams and visions didn't die with the apostles, or fulfillment of the cannon of scriptures. The eastern culture still accepts dreams more than the western culture, which values intellect and deductive learning over inductive learning.

Dreams had a distinct place before Christ and in early church history. God's been speaking to mankind, believers and non-believers, throughout history through dreams and visions. Why would we limit God in how He can speak to us today?

We need to study dream interpretation God's way to know and hear what He is saying to His church, His people. (Rev. 2:7, 11, 17, 29 & 3:6, 13, 22); He who has an ear, let him hear what the Spirit says to the churches.

As we see and hear what the Father is doing, we come to know our God, and His heart. We join Him, doing divine exploits. (Dan. 11:32) God is raising up a people who know God intimately, and who will be transformed into His likeness by beholding and becoming like Him.

But we all, with unveiled face, beholding as in a mirror the glory of the Lord, are being transformed into the same image from glory to glory, just as from the Lord, the Spirit.
2 Cor. 3:18 (NASB)

DREAMS COME FROM THREE SOURCES

1. God, the Holy Spirit

Then being divinely warned in a dream that they should not return to Herod, they departed for their own country another way.

Matt. 2:12 (NKJV)

2. Natural Man

Thus says the Lord of hosts: "Do not listen to the words of the prophets who prophesy to you. They make you worthless; They speak a vision of their own heart, not from the mouth of the Lord."

Jer. 23:16 (NKJV)

3. The Demonic Realm

Now it happened, as we went to prayer, that a certain slave girl possessed with a spirit of divination met us, who brought her masters much profit by fortune-telling.

Acts 16:16 (NKJV)

Chapter 5

DREAM TYPES FROM GOD THE
HOLY SPIRIT

DREAMS FROM GOD, THE HOLY SPIRIT

1. Warning dreams

These dreams may offer protection and guidance. God warned Laban, the wise men, Joseph, and Pilate's wife in dreams.

"I have the power to harm you, but last night the God of your father said to me, 'Be careful not to say anything to Jacob either good or bad.'"
Gen. 31:29 (NIV)

Then being divinely warned in a dream that they should not return to Herod, they departed for their own country another way.
Matt. 2:12 (NKJV)

Now when Herod was dead, behold, an angel of the Lord appeared in a dream to Joseph in Egypt, saying, "Arise, take the young Child and His mother, and go to the land of Israel for those who sought the young Child's life are dead." Then he arose, took the young Child and His mother, and came into the land of Israel. But when he heard that Archelaus was reigning over Judea instead of his father Herod, he was afraid to go there. And being warned by God in a dream, he turned aside into the region of Galilee. And he came and dwelt in a city called Nazareth, that it might be fulfilled which was spoken by the prophets, "He shall be called a Nazarene."
Matt. 2:19-23 (NKJV)

While he was sitting on the judgment seat, his wife sent to him, saying, "Have nothing to do with that just Man, for I have suffered many things today in a dream because of Him,"
Matt. 27:19 (NKJV)

2. Calling / Destiny dreams

Calling dreams are destiny dreams that reveal part of God's calling and purpose regarding your life, guidance, and vocation. Generally they relate to your sphere of influence.

Sometimes they will be extrinsic dreams regarding God's redemptive plan for a city, region, or nation.

Sometimes destiny dreams are more personal and reveal the unfolding of God's plan in your life. They may relate to the present, the past, or the future.

Abraham's calling dream was literal, and Joseph's calling dream was metaphorical.

Then the Lord said to him, "Know for certain that for four hundred years your descendants will be strangers in a country not their own and they will be enslaved and mistreated there. But I will punish the nation they serve as slaves, and afterward they will come out with great possessions. You, however will go to your fathers in peace and be buried at a good old age. In the fourth generation your descendants will come back here, for the sin of the Amorites has not yet reached its full measure."
Gen. 15:13-15 (NIV)

He said to them, "Please listen to this dream which I have had; for behold, we were binding sheaves in the field, and lo, my sheaf rose up and also stood erect; and behold, your sheaves gathered around and bowed down to my sheaf."

Now he had still another dream, and related it to his brothers, and said, "Lo, I have had still another dream, and behold, the sun and the moon and eleven stars were bowing down to me."
Gen. 37:6, 9 (NASB)

3. Directional Dreams

Directive dreams often contain a higher level of revelation and are prophetic in nature. Their purpose is to give specific guidance, which may even include warnings of some kind.

Directional dreams serve to help you get farther down the road toward fulfilling your destiny and purpose, showing you signposts and helping you avoid pitfalls along the way. An example is found in Matt. 2 in the dream of the wise men being warned by God to not return to Herod.

4. Creative Dreams

Creative dreams involve such things as designs, inventions, and new ways of doing things. God often uses creative dreams with artistic people to give them songs to sing, pictures to paint, or words to write. Handel's Messiah and Einstein's theory of relativity are said to have been given in dreams.

Jacob had a dream of how to increase his wages from Laban.

> *"In breeding season I once had a dream in which I looked up and saw that the male goats mating with the flock were streaked, speckled or spotted."*
> **Gen. 31:10 (NIV)**

When Joseph interpreted Pharaoh's dreams, God gave wisdom of how to prepare for the years of famine.

> *Then Pharaoh said to Joseph, Since God has made all this known to you, there is no one so discerning and wise as you.*
> **Gen 41:39 (NIV)**

5. Self- Condition Dreams

These dreams show you where you presently stand with God and reveal the heart. Sin is revealed with conviction, not condemnation. They show the error of your ways.

These self-condition dreams are preferred ways of correction. It's between you and God. It's important to respond to the correction to prevent further God correction or discipline.

But God came to Abimelek in a dream one night and said to him, "You are as good as dead because of the woman you have taken; she is a married woman."
Gen. 20:3 (NIV)

6. Exhortation Dreams

These dreams confirm what God is saying, offer courage and may contain a strong sense of urgency. They may answer questions you've been asking the Lord. They may reveal an accurate, detailed picture of what is going on behind the scenes, especially in the demonic realm. They produce faith and challenge you to take action regarding the revelation.

When Gideon heard the dream and its interpretation, he bowed down and worshipped. He returned to the camp of Israel and called out, "Get up! The Lord has given the Midianite camp into your hands.
Judg. 7:15 (NIV)

7. Comfort / Healing / Deliverance Dreams

These dreams can bring forgiveness, love, healing and deliverance. These dreams help to heal you of past emotions and memories by giving you God's perspective on a situation. The dream Gideon heard in Judges 7:13, brought deliverance to Israel.

8. Revelation / Instruction Dreams

God reveals His plans, spiritual insights and instruction in dreams. Scriptures are often highlighted and you may hear a voice speaking to you.

But after he had considered this, an angel of the Lord appeared to him in a dxream and said, "Joseph son of David, do not be afraid to take Mary home as your wife, because what is conceived in her is from the Holy Spirit.
Matt. 1:20 (NIV)

9. Prophetic Dreams

These dreams reveal the future and may be more literal than figurative. Abraham's dream revealed the future for him and his descendants.

> *Then the Lord said to him, "Know for certain that for four hundred years your descendants will be strangers in a country not their own and they will be enslaved and mistreated there. But I will punish the nation they serve as slaves, and afterward they will come out with great possessions. You, however will go to your fathers in peace and be buried at a good old age. In the fourth generation your descendants will come back here, for the sin of the Amorites has not yet reached its full measure."*
> **Gen. 15:13-15 (NIV)**

10. Intercession Dreams

These are dreams that God gives you to pray for someone or for future problems. Dreams from the Holy Spirit will be according to the calling of God on your life and according to the sphere of influence you have in your life. Examples include earthquake dreams.

11. Cleansing /Flushing Dreams

One of the most common images associated with the cleansing dream is that of being in the bathroom, on the toilet, or taking a shower. Cleansing dreams are used to wash you from the dust and dirt picked up by walking in the world. The blood of Jesus is cleansing your heart and mind from evil you have come in contact with.

12. Spiritual Warfare Dreams

Spiritual warfare dreams are calls to prayer that reveal hindrances and strongholds need to be torn down. These dreams may be black and white and reveal the attacks coming against you or others. They usually involve some sort of life or death feeling. God is revealing to you the plans of the enemy. They are given to make you aware of the enemy's plans so that you may pray and act contrary to the plans.

Chapter 6

DREAM TYPES FROM THE NATURAL MAN

DREAMS FROM MAN

1. Body dreams

These dreams generally arise from and reflect some aspect of the physical condition of the person who is dreaming. These dreams can come from physical sickness, pregnancy, or chemicals. Drugs and alcohol can cause nightmares as the body adjusts back to normal.

2. Soul dreams

These dreams can simply be emotions expressing your needs or desires, or they can be born out of your fleshly desires. When you are born again, God renews and breaks old mindsets and strongholds of the soul, so your spirit man can grow. Dreams are influenced according to the level you have submitted your soul to the Holy Spirit to rule in your life. An example of a soul dream would be of desiring a specific mate and being convinced he/she is to marry you.

God gives dreams to accomplish a function. If you think you know what the dream means, but don't know why God gave the dream, you may have missed the meaning of the dream. Ask the question why did God give this dream?

DREAM TYPES FROM THE
DEMONIC REALMS
Chapter 7

Anything that God has and uses, the enemy seeks to counterfeit, including dreams.

FALSE DREAMS/ DECEPTIVE DREAMS

Deceptive dreams are often the work of deceitful spirits, which Scripture says will be particularly active in the last days. (1Tim.4:1) Deceptive spirits seek to draw us away from a place of security to a place of insecurity. Deceptive dreams create images and impressions in your mind that will turn from the true path of God's light into the darkness of error and heresy.

By using scripture and support from the Body of Christ, one can reject the enemy's plans, and flip them for what God's purposes are.

> *The idols speak deceitfully, diviners see visions that lie; they tell dreams that are false, they give comfort in vain. Therefore the people wander like sheep oppressed for lack of a shepherd.*
> **Zech. 10:2 (NIV)**

> *Yes, this is what the Lord almighty, the God of Israel says: "Do not let the prophets and diviners among you deceive you. Do not listen to the dreams you encourage them to have."*
> **Jer. 29:8 (NIV)**

1. Fear dreams

Most nightmares, especially childhood nightmares, fall into this category. Dreams of fear and panic often arise from trauma. Simply rebuking the fear or the panic may not be enough. It may be necessary to ask the Holy Spirit to reveal the root of the frightening dreams so that repentance, cleansing, or healing can take place.

Your fear opens you up to things that you fear. Learn to exercise your authority in Christ and ward off these haunting dreams in Jesus' name. You empower what you focus on.

2. Dark Dreams

These dreams can be dark in mood and tone and with subdued or muted colors. The lack of bright lively colors is one way of determining that a dream may come from a dark or demonic source.

Dark dreams commonly conjure up dark emotions and often employ dark symbols that instill a sense of discomfort. Illegal drug use and involvement with witchcraft can open up one to dark dreams.

INTERPRETATION OF DREAMS, VISIONS AND
NIGHT VISIONS

Dreams and visions are similar except generally a dream occurs during periods of sleep, while a vision generally refers to images or revelations received in picture form while a person is awake. You can have a dream while awake and you can have a vision while asleep. (Example in Gen. 15, Abraham's dream was actually a vision). In fact, the dreams, which seem so real and you remember so well, may actually be visions.

DREAMS

Dreams are defined as a succession of picture like images, events and dialogue that a person receives or experiences during the sleep state of unconsciousness. Dreams are God's night parables or symbolic picture language. Dreams are formed in the subconscious mind of a person based on images and symbols, which are unique to the individual depending on his or her background, experience and current life circumstances. Dreams are messages sent either from God's Spirit or from your own soul comprised of your mind, will and emotions. Spiritual dreams are inspired by God, and then communicated to our subconscious minds bypassing the resistance of our conscious minds and soul (mind, will and emotions). Dreams can communicate to us truth that our conscious mind may have failed to acknowledge the truth. One word for dream in Greek is enupnion, which means "something seen in sleep or a vision during sleep." (Acts 2:17; Jude 1:8)

VISIONS

Visions are defined as "the act or power of perceiving abstract or invisible subjects as clearly as if they were visible objects." Visions reveal images, pictures or short dreams that are introduced into the conscious mind or trance state, which is not actually present at that time and place. A vision is also defined as "foresight". One Arabic word for vision

is chizzayown, which means "a revelation especially by a dream. (2 Sam. 7:17; Job 4:13; Isa. 22:1; Zech. 13:4) A Greek word, horasis, is translated as vision in the New Testament and means "something gazed at, a sight, a thing seen."(Matt. 17:9, Acts 7:31 & 9:10, 12)

1. Visions seem so real that they can be hard to distinguish from real life.
2. Visions are God's way of making Himself known to us. The Lord said to Aaron and Miriam.

He said, "Hear now My words: If there is a prophet among you, I, the Lord, shall make myself known to him in a vision. I shall speak with him in a dream. "Not so with my servant Moses, He is faithful in all My household; with him, I speak mouth to mouth, even openly, and not in dark sayings, and he beholds the form of the Lord. Why then were you not afraid to speak against My servant, against Moses?"

Num. 12:6-8 (NASB)

3. Visions are the picture language of God.
4. Visions are usually received while awake during times of worship, prayer, meditation, fasting, contemplation or even when you least expect it. (ex. Shawn Bolz had a vision while playing video games)
5. Visions can come at night while sleeping. The dreams that you really remember and seem real may be night visions.
6. Visions will be etched and burned in your spirit.

TWO WAYS VISIONS ARE SEEN

1. Internally

They can be seen in the mind's eye, or inner eye, can be at night. King Nebuchadnezzar had visions at night that terrified him (Dan. 4:5, 10, 13). This was King Nebuchadnezzar's dream of a tree. Daniel had a vision at night internally of the four beasts that terrified him (Dan. 7:7). These dreams were very real and would be called night visions.

2. Externally

They can be seen with the eyes wide open in three ways:

a. Co-existing spiritual realm.
i) For example, Elisha's servant's eyes were opened to see the army of God in horses and chariots of fire. (2 Kings 6:17)

b. Open heaven experience
i) Ezekiel, Isaiah, and Jacob saw an open heaven and gazed upon the throne of God. (Ezek. 1:1; Isa. 6; Gen. 28:12)

c. The future realm
i) Daniel saw visions of the future with open-eyes. (Dan. 8:3 & 10:7)

ii) The apostle John also saw visions in the book of Revelation.

iii) During visions, the spiritual realm is opened to us.

iv) In visions, the external realm is seen. No time exists in that realm.

Chapter 9

LUCID
DREAMING
AND HEALING PRAYER

Lucid dreaming simply means you know you are dreaming. "Lucid Dreaming" was coined by Frederik Van Eeden from the Netherlands, who was a psychiatrist and writer in the late 19th century and early 20th century. Though he was influenced by Hindu ideas of selfhood and Boehme's mysticism, he was a Roman Catholic and gave lucid dreaming its name. Lucid Dreaming has come to mean having mental clarity while one is sleeping. Lucid dreaming occurs when a dreamer realizes he/ she is sleeping. It is a skill dreamers are able to develop and enables them to interpret their dreams while sleeping.

Through lucid dreaming, the dreamer is able to interact with his dream while dreaming, and become the creator in the dream and not the victim. If the dreamer doesn't like something in a dream, he can change it by inviting Jesus to come into his dream and by taking the authority he has as a child of the King of Kings. As one becomes skilled in dream interpretation, and recognizes a demon coming after him in a dream, he can simply command the demon to leave in the name of Jesus, or simply "think" Jesus and the demon must leave. In many of my workshops, people have found freedom and healing in knowing and applying lucid dreaming to their dream life.

Since dreams are spirit, one can re-enter his dreams while awake. In prayer ministry, often a client's dream reveals the issues in his / her life needing prayer. The dreamer asks the Lord if we can re-enter his dream. I will only enter a dream, after the dreamer has asked and received permission by the Lord Jesus. I do this because I don't want to go anywhere in the Spiritual Realm without going through the door of Jesus. After entering the dream, I will encourage the dreamer, to take back what the enemy has stolen, cast demons out of his house or vehicle, and close any doors of his house or car, that have allowed enemy access to his life.

I have witnessed hundreds being set free of captivity and it all began with a God inspired dream and an understanding of how to respond to it. Through prayer, and re-entering the dream through the door of Jesus, the dreamer can be set free to lead a victorious Christian life. All the glory goes to Jesus. Many have received healing and victory in their lives. Transformation begins with a dream.

Chapter 10

DREAMS IN
HEALING PRAYER

Dreams can be used in healing prayer because they reveal issues that the Lord is revealing which need to be dealt with. In sleep, the conscious mind is bypassed, and there is less resistance to the truth. Our heavenly Father will use dreams and visions as an avenue of identifying the obstacles that hinder your path to walking out His purposes in your life.

In prayer ministry, we often ask the person requesting prayer to ask God to remind him of a dream that He would like us to look at. Often the one requesting prayer had a dream the night before that is significant. I love it when God sets things up for a person desiring healing. Other times, the Lord will remind the person of a dream he had as a child, or a reoccurring dream that is significant. These dreams will usually reveal the issues the person needs prayer for. The revealed issues often have generational roots or roots in traumatic events that happened in the person's childhood.

Dreams reveal the issues in the soul and spirit that need healing. God is shining His light on the issue needing prayer, and directs how to pray for healing. By following God's direction, I have seen people healed of issues that have bothered them for over 25 years simply by praying a 15 minute prayer. If a sin issue is revealed, the dreamer repents and renounces his sin and generational iniquity, inviting the blood of Jesus to wash away the sin and iniquity. If the dreamer was a victim, often forgiveness is needed for the perpetrator, so the dreamer can be set free from all ungodly soul ties holding him captive. If the dreamer came into agreement with the lies of the enemy, these lies need to be renounced. Judgments and ungodly vows need to be renounced, and repentance needs to be made for bitterness and resentment.

In trauma and abuse, the victim through agreement with the lies of the enemy, can be taken to the pit, Sheol, the depth, and ungodly dimensional places of captivity. People have described seeing themselves held in caves, glass containers, tombs, closets, and

dark dimensional places. Through prayer, we invite the light of Jesus to come in, and to shine His glory light in this dark dimensional place and on the soul wound. We pray that the Lord brings the wounded soul out of the ungodly depth or dimensional place of captivity. Sometimes, there is a child-part of the person that breaks agreement with the lie of the enemy holding him captive, and invites Jesus to come and rescue him from the dark place. We ask Jesus to wash, heal and cleanse this child-part or wounded soul from all the hurt and abuse and to take him to a heavenly place to be healed and restored. After restoration, we ask the Lord to reunite the child part to the adult and to shine His glory light on the soul wound and bring it to complete healing.

In prayer ministry, I am so often amazed at how God desires healing for everyone and one of the ways He reveals the issues at hand is through dreams, visions, and images. By asking the Lord questions, and following the leading of the Holy Spirit, in prayer ministry, I've seen dramatic results and healing in people. Many times it began with simply asking the Lord to remind him of a dream that we are to look at.

Chapter 11

TYPES, SPHERES, CATEGORIES OF
DREAMS & VISIONS

VISION VS. DREAMS

Generally speaking, visions are considered to be literal, and therefore no interpretation is needed. Dreams, on the other hand, are metaphorical, and like night parables, they need to be interpreted.

For example, the book of Revelation is in picture form. God will speak to you using symbols and vocabulary you are familiar with. For example, Lou Engle had dreams of basketball courts, which meant to him, the judicial courts. You will develop your own dream language with the Lord.

THERE ARE THREE TYPES OF DREAMS

1. A simple message dream

These dreams are clearly understood, direct, and to the point. The interpretation is literal. An example is Joseph's dream to take Mary as his wife (Matt. 1:20).

2. The simple symbolic dream

These dreams have metaphors and symbols. The symbols are from the dreamer's dream language or from scripture. An example of this is Joseph's dreams in Genesis 37 regarding the brother's sheaves of wheat bowing down to his sheave of wheat, and the sun, the moon, and the eleven stars bowing down to him. Jacob, Joseph's father, responded to Joseph's dream, with, "Shall you mother and I and your brothers indeed come to bow down to the earth before you?"

3. The complex symbolic dream

This type of dream needs revelation for interpretation which comes from the Holy Spirit and skill developed by practice and experience. An example of this is Pharaoh's dream about the (7) seven fat cows and the (7) seven skinny cows eating up the fat cows and (7) seven withered heads of grain devouring (7) seven full grains that Joseph interpreted.

SPHERES OF DREAMS

Dreams and visions allow us to be in two or more dimensions simultaneously. We can travel to the past or to the future. We can transcend age – we can be in our childhood home and at our current age. We may even find ourselves looking through someone else's eyes as if we were viewing things from inside him or her. We can travel at the speed of light.

Dreams move us about intra-dimensionally and seem to change matter into energy and turn chaos into order. God can point out through a dream when you need to correct and bring yourself into alignment.

CATEGORIES OF DREAMS

1. Intrinsic Dreams

This category encompasses the vast majority of most people's dreams. Most dreams are about oneself. God gives us personal dreams of self-disclosure in order to help us on life's journey. These are dreams that deal with heart issues that pertain to matters of our soul, personal longings, opinions, and emotions.

2. Extrinsic Dreams

These dreams focus on something or someone other than you. Only 1-5% of most people's dreams are extrinsic in nature. The greater our intimacy with the Lord, the more extrinsic dreams we have. An example of this is in Pharaoh's dreams (Gen. 41:32).

External dreams relate to your sphere of influence. Sometimes these dreams will be used to call you to something but not fully release or commission you into it. In this case, think of the dreams as part of your learning curve, your training in

your spiritual vocabulary. God shows you a glimpse what lies ahead in order to whet your appetite and inspire you to continue pressing forward. The most common purpose of external dreams is to draw us into intercession. Generally intercessors or those in spiritual leadership have more extrinsic dreams.

Chapter 12

SECULAR VS. BIBLICAL INTERPRETATION

Two people in the Bible were dream interpreters, Daniel and Joseph. They studied dream interpretation of the popular method of the day. Daniel was trained by the Babylonian wise men of the day. Joseph was acquainted with the Egyptian methods of interpretation. However, God gave them knowledge and skill.

Joseph recognized that dream interpretation came from God.

> *Then they said to him, "We have had a dream and there is no one to interpret it." Then Joseph said to them, "Do not interpretations belong to God? Tell it to me please."*
> *Gen. 40:8 (NASB)*

The popular method of the day could not interpret the dream then and the same is true today. Dreams from God cannot be interpreted by the popular psychological methods of today. In short, the main differences between the secular and Biblical dream interpretation is that secular interpretation is soul based, self-focused, and introspective while the Biblical interpretation is spirit based, God centered, and theospective. In Biblical interpretation, there can be levels of meanings and the dreamer's spirit is the judge of the interpretation. In contrast, in a secular interpretation, there is a single interpretation and the counselor/ therapist is the sole judge of the interpretation. The Jungian and Freudian methods of today cannot interpret a dream from God.

JUNGIAN DREAM ANALYSIS

Dreams depict aspects of the dreamer's personality that have been neglected in his or her conscious life in order to attempt to reveal the subconscious. Everything in the dream is about you; for example, a baby is your inner child.

They believe that things on the inside are working its way out versus the Biblical approach that things on the outside are working its way in.

The approach identifies Archetypes – like the masculine, feminine, or Mandala (shadowy) side of a person. The theory uses mythology, history, and comparative religions. The dreamer is asked what conscious attitude does the dream compensate? Does the dream reveal unconscious prejudices, attitudes, conflicts and desires?

Carl Jung is not a Christian. By accepting these principles in dream interpretation, the church is allowing pagan and occult thinking to enter the church.

FREUDIAN DREAM ANALYSIS

Dreams come from memories that are stimulated by unconscious wishes, which have their origins in our childhood. It doesn't matter whether the patient agrees or feels the interpretation is correct, because the patient is not aware of his or her subconscious thoughts or feelings. Dreams are full of sexually erotic overtones and the focus is on latent unconscious feelings of which dreamers aren't aware.

In the psychotherapy models, everything in the dream represents a piece of you. If you use that method to interpret King Nebuchadnezzar's statue dream of the head being gold, the breast being silver, the thighs being bronze and the legs being iron and clay, one would say he had major childhood issues.

INTERPRETATIONS FROM GOD

Interpretation comes from God, so ask the Lord for help in interpretation. Dreams come first to our subconscious mind and later when we are aware of them, come to our conscious minds. Because of the divine nature of revelation, we must depend on the Holy Spirit for understanding.

Then they said to him, "We have had a dream and there is no one to interpret it." Then Joseph said to them, "Do not interpretations belong to God? Tell it to me, please. "
Gen. 40:8, (NASB)

"I will ask the Father, and He will give you another Helper, that He may be with you forever."
John 14:16 (NASB)

"But the Helper, the Holy Spirit, whom the Father will send in My name, He will teach you all things, and bring to your remembrance all that I said to you."
John 14:26 (NASB)

"But when He, the Spirit of truth, comes, He will guide you into all the truth; for He will not speak on His own initiative, but whatever He hears, He will speak; and He will disclose to you what will come. He will glorify Me, for He will take of Mine and will disclose it to you."

John 16:13-15 (NASB)

The Holy Spirit has been sent to reveal the revelations of God to us. He is our Helper, our Tutor, and our Friend.

We have to rely on the Holy Spirit for interpretation. It's more than just having the necessary tools to interpret dreams. Without God's help, we will not be able to understand dreams. There are no pat answers or fixed rules for dream interpretation. God will not remove our need for the Holy Spirit. We can have revelatory gifting, but we need skill in dream interpretation. Without study, one is only correct as how well he/she hears from God. For more accuracy, combine the mechanics of dream interpretation and the Holy Spirit.

Chapter 13

INTERPRETATION
PRINCIPLES

GOD MAY CHOOSE TO GIVE THE INTERPRETATION IN ONE OF FOUR WAYS

1. **By instantaneously revealing a dream's meaning through an angel, as God did with Daniel.**

2. **By simultaneously speaking the dream's interpretation to us as we sleep.**

3. **By the process of writing it down.**

    "All this," said David, "the LORD made me understand in writing by His hand upon me, all the details of this pattern."
    1 Chron. 28:19 (NASB)

4. **By unfolding a dream's meaning as you mature in understanding His ways.**

    "All this," said David, "the LORD made me understand in writing by His hand upon me, all the details of this pattern."
    1 Chron. 28:19 (NASB)

    a. God will hide things from you until an appropriate time.

    b. God places great value on your searching for the things He conceals. It's God's love language, so you will choose to spend time with Him.

    c. Often you learn as much if not more in the discovery process of interpreting a dream as you do in simply obtaining the dream's answer itself.

INTUITIVE DREAM RECORDING

1. **Learn to write beyond straight lines.**

2. **Forget grammar, sentences, and paragraphs.**

3. **Name, date, and title your dream. The title should be the focus of the dream.**

4. **Write your dream out in a diagram, outline or paragraph form.**

   Then they said to him, "We have had a dream and there is no one to interpret it." Then Joseph said to them, "Do not interpretations belong to God? Tell it to me please."
   Gen. 40:8 (NASB)

   a. It releases right-brain thinking.

   b. It clarifies the focus or theme.

   c. It enriches the dream by drawing out details

   d. It helps to un-stick linear thought patterns.

5. **Record the main facts and eliminate the unnecessary details.**

6. **Different Methods**

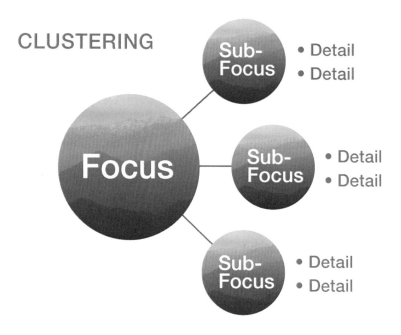

FLOW CHART – HIERARCHICAL

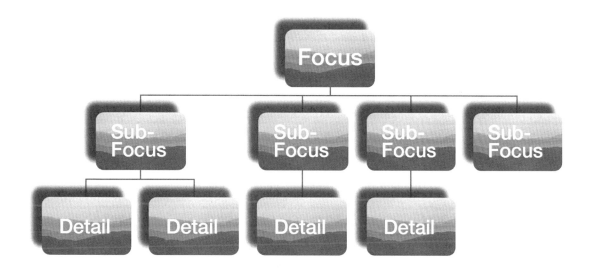

DIAGRAMMING

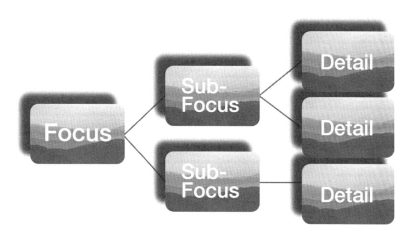

REMEMBERING DREAMS

Dreams images are written in our minds with disappearing ink. If we don't re-experience them immediately, dreams become invisible.

1. **Try to wake up slowly and capture the twilight time when you hear God speak.**

2. **Ask the Holy Spirit to wake you up before your alarm clock does.**

3. **Immediately go over the dream with God and write down any dreams.**

INTERPRETATION TIPS

1. **Ask God for understanding.**

2. **Study the parables of Jesus.**

3. **View dreams the same way as parables.**

4. **Refer to Scripture.**

5. **Develop a dream vocabulary.**

6. **Note colloquial expressions, idioms, and puns Examples: serving (in tennis), C section, court.**

7. **Ask what the symbol means to you.**

8. **Make a note of your feelings in the dream.**

9. **Get counsel from gifted interpreters, not necessarily friends.**

INTERPRETATION BASICS

1. **Enter the dream with the Lord Jesus' permission.**

2. **Ask, if the dreamer is a participant or an observer.**

3. **Note the colors.**

4. **Find the focus and sub focuses.**

5. Think metaphorically. Find the key metaphor.

6. Look for contrasts. Why this and not that?

7. Keep the main things, the main things.

8. Why did God give the dreamer the dream?

9. Interpret the dream in 2-3 sentences.

ESTABLISH THE FOCUS AND SUB FOCUS

1. The focus is who or what the dream is about.

2. Ask who is this dream about? What's the center of attention?

3. If you can remove an element and the dream falls apart, that was the focus.

4. Sub-focuses are the elements in a dream that are necessary to find the theme / plot of the dream and to make it have meaning.

5. Ask would this dream be the same without this element?

6. What did this particular element add to the whole of the dream?

INTERPRETIVE PROCESS

1. Visualize the dream as you recall or rehearse the main symbols in the scenes of the dream story. Enter back into the dream again. God will give you more revelation as you revisit the dream.

2. Ask what part the dreamer has in the dream. Are you an observer, a participant or the main focus?

3. Ask what are the colors - bright, muted tones or black and white?

4. Find the focus and sub focus.

5. Keep the main thing, the main thing.

6. Reduce the dream to its simplest form.

7. Look at the context of the dream.

8. Determine the tone of the dream. Determine the emotions, attitudes and agendas of those in the dream.

9. Where did the dream take place?

WHAT IS THE SETTING?

10. Is it set in the past, present or future tense?

11. Look at the context of the dream.

12. Ask the Holy Spirit for insight and understanding of the dream through biblical imagery.

13. Does the dream symbol appear in the Bible? Look at the symbols collectively as they correlate to each other.

14. Ask thought provoking questions. What is highlighted to you? Go into dialogue with Holy Spirit. Why is it this symbol and not that? Ask the Lord, and then listen. Expect an encounter with the Lord.

15. Look for the theme or essence the dream is communicating to you. What type of dream is this? Why did God give this dream?

Chapter 14

MOST COMMON
DREAMS

1. Dreams of your House

The house normally represents the individual's life and circumstances taking place in the house reflect specific activity in the dreamer's life. These dreams may also represent the dreamer's family or place of worship. Note the context and people in the dream.

2. Dreams of Going to School

The dreamer may be learning something new. Often these dreams include taking tests. This can be a dream of going through a test for the purpose of promotion. Classes or tests might need to be retaken. This may indicate that something important wasn't learned earlier and is being taught again.

3. Dreams of Being Chased or Chasing

These dreams often reveal enemies that are at work coming against your life and purpose. The enemy is trying to generate and empower fear. Note the context of the dream and the emotion. The dream may show a passionate pursuit for God or from God in the dreamer's life.

4. Dreams of Flying

God is communicating to the person that he or she has an ability to move in the spirit realm and rise above problems. These dreams can be highly inspirational.

5. Dreams of Various Vehicles

These dreams may indicate the calling the dreamer has, his ministry his vocation, or his purpose in life. Note the size and type of vehicle. Cars, planes, buses, bicycles, etc. may be symbols of the type and even the size of the ministry a person is or will be engaged in.

6. Dreams Concerning Storms

These are often hints of things that are on the horizon. If the color of the storm is light or bright, it refers to something God is bringing. If the color of the storm is dark or muted, it is speaking about negative or destructive forces from powers of darkness.

7. Dreams of Being Naked or Exposed

These dreams indicate that the dreamer will be or is becoming transparent and vulnerable. These can be fearful.

8. Dreams about Teeth

Are the teeth loose, falling out, rotten, or shining? These dreams have to do with the dreamer's ability to comprehend or understand. If the teeth are falling out, God is communicating the need or inability to understand and discern something. Which tooth is the focus? Eyeteeth have to do with revelation and wisdom teeth have to do with wisdom.

9. Dreams of Past Relationships

These might indicate that the person is being tempted to fall back into old patterns and ways of thinking. Note who the person is and what he or she represents to the dreamer.

10. Dreams of Dying

These dreams are not usually literal about the person seen in the dream but are symbolic about something that is passing away or departing from the dreamer's life. Note who the person is and what he or she represents to him / her. The person may reveal an issue, era, or career that is coming to an end.

11. Dreams of Relatives Alive and Dead

These dreams, especially if of grandparents, probably indicate generational issues at work in the dreamer's life either blessings or curses. Discernment will be needed on whether to receive the blessings or cut off the curses.

12. Dreams of Births /Babies

Usually these dreams are not literal, but rather about a new gift, calling, purpose or ministry coming forth into the life of the dreamer. Note if a name is given to the child.

13. Dreams of Cleansing

Bathroom dreams (toilet, showers, and baths) indicate that God is cleansing an area of the dreamer's life, or removing some things that have negatively affected the dreamer or that could impact the dreamer's future.

14. Dreams of Falling

These dreams may reveal that there is a fear of losing control of some area of life or that the dreamer is getting free of directing his / her own life. Note the results of the fall and the emotions felt which will help to interpret the dream.

15. Dreams of Going through Doors, Closing Doors, or Stairways

These dreams reveal change is coming through new ways, new opportunities, and new advancements, or there is an entry into the dreamer's life for the enemy that needs to be closed. Dreams with stairs and elevators going up indicate the dreamer is coming up higher in his /her purpose and calling while going down would mean the opposite, and a warning.

16. Dreams of Wild Animals

The most common is snake dreams, which reveal the serpent – the devil with His demonic hosts at work through accusation, lying attacks. Alligators indicate that someone with great influence has launched a verbal attack or spread gossip that is hidden and dangerous. Similarly, spiders indicate something the dreamer is involved in is negatively affecting his or her life.

17. Dreams of Domesticated Animals

Dogs usually represent friendship, loyalty, companionship, and protection. If the dog is growling, attacking, or biting, these dreams could reveal a friend who is about to betray you. Cat dreams vary depending upon what cats mean to the dreamer. If a personal pet, it could be something or someone dear to the dreamer. Otherwise, it could represent independent thinking, persnickety attitudes and even the occult. Horses represent power and authority. Color is important.

18. Dreams of Clocks and Watches

These dreams reveal what time it is in the dreamer's life or the need for a wakeup call in the body of Christ or nation. It's time to be alert and watchful. These dreams might indicate a scripture verse as well as give a deeper message.

19. Dreams of Losing Your Purse /Wallet

God is communicating that the dreamer has lost or is looking for his or her purpose, identity, and favor.

20. Dreams Called Nightmares

These are common with children and new believers, and are caused by the enemy for intimidation, to dull spiritual sensitivity, and to induce fear and rejection of spiritual things, particularly dreams. These may reveal generational enemies at work that need to be cut off.

As you seek out God's secret language, He will speak to you in your own dream language. He uses dark speech in metaphors, puns, riddles, alliterations, symbols and types.

BASIC SYMBOLS AND TYPES

1. **Type - It is the shape, style or resemblance of that which is to come.**

   Nevertheless death reigned from Adam to Moses, even over those who had not sinned according to the likeness of the transgression of Adam, who is a type of Him who was to come.
   Rom. 5:14 (NKJV)

2. **Symbol - It is something that represents someone or something; 1 Cor. 11:10 (head covering- symbol of authority)**.

3. **Pattern - It is the exact way something should be done or made.**

   Make this tabernacle and all its furnishings exactly like the pattern I will show you.
   Ex. 25:9 (NIV)

4. **Shadow - It is to prefigure that which is to come.**

   So let no one judge you in food or in drink, or regarding a festival or a new moon or sabbaths, which are a shadow of things to come, but the substance is of Christ.
   Col. 2:16-17 (NKJV)

5. **Sign - It is a signal, evidence of that which is coming, earthly oriented.**

And God said to Noah, "This is the sign of the covenant which I have established between Me and all flesh that is on the earth."
Gen. 9:17 (NKJV)

6. **Wonder - A conspicuous miracle that validates what is coming, heavenly oriented.**

   I will show wonders in heaven above and signs in the earth beneath: Blood and fire and vapor of smoke.
   Acts 2:19 (NKJV)

7. **Parable - It is a fictitious narrative that illustrates a parallel truth.**

   "Therefore I speak to them in parables, because seeing they do not see, and hearing they do not hear, nor do they understand."
   Matt. 13:13 (NKJV)

8. **Simile - It is a comparison using "like" or "as"**

   The hair on his head was white like wool, as white as snow, and his eyes were like blazing fire. His feet were like bronze glowing in a furnace, and his voice was like the sound of rushing waters.
   Rev. 1:14-15 (NIV)

9. **Metaphor - It is a comparison without using "like" or "as".**

   Then Jesus said to them again, "Most assuredly, I say to you, I am the door of the sheep.
   John 10:7 (NKJV)

The disciples had forgotten to bring bread, except for one loaf they had with them in the boat. "Be careful," Jesus warned them. "Watch out for the yeast of the Pharisees and that of Herod." They discussed this with one another and said, "It is because we have no bread." Aware of their discussion, Jesus asked them: "Why are you talking about having no bread? Do you still not see or understand? Are your hearts hardened? Do you have eyes but fail to see, and ears but fail to hear? And don't you remember? When I broke the five loaves for the five thousand, how many basketfuls of pieces did you pick up?"

"Twelve," they replied. He said to them, "Do you still not understand?"
Mark 8:14–19, 21 (NIV)

Question: What do the door and the yeast represent?

THREE PLACES TO FIND SYMBOLS

1. Scripture

Search the scriptures to see how a particular symbol is used. You will need to determine if the symbol in your dream is good or bad. For example, a lion in scripture can be the lion of Judah or it can be Satan seeking to devour. Which kind of lion was in your dream?

2. Colloquial Expressions

God takes the sayings, idioms, and puns that you are familiar with and uses them to speak spiritual truth.

For example (Judg. 7:13-14) when Gideon heard the Midianite's dream, of the barley loaf knocking down a tent, he was encouraged because it was known that the barley loaf (inferior grain) represented Israel and the tent represented Midian (a nomadic tribe).

3. Your personal dream language

What a symbol means to you, may mean something different to someone else. Note what role the symbol plays and what it is doing in the dream. For example, dogs may mean something good to one person (a friend), but to another something bad (an enemy). As you record your dreams, you will gradually become familiar to your dream language.

ASK QUESTIONS ABOUT THE ANIMALS IN THE DREAM

1. Is the animal domesticated or undomesticated?

2. Did I feel afraid or threatened by this animal?

3. What action did the animal play in the dream?

4. What are the characteristics of the animal in nature?

5. Is the animal my pet?

DOMESTICATED ANIMALS

1. Cat – (-) Independent spirit; could be witchcraft; (+) If a personal pet, someone dear to you.

2. Dog - Loyal friend or companion, or enemy with a biting temper; devourer (1 King 21).

3. Horse - Powerful ministry; note the color.

4. Birds - What kind? Good or bad? (+) Dove - The Holy Spirit; (-) Black Birds - Steal the word, but ravens fed Elijah.

5. Pig – Not born again, stuck in the mire, unclean.

6. Cow – Provision, giver of milk or meat. Pharaoh's dream (Gen. 41).

7. Rooster - Time to wake up; new beginnings, alarm

UNDOMESTICATED ANIMALS

1. Lion – (+) King of the beasts, King of Judah; or (-) Satan seeking to devour.

2. Eagle - Prophet or eagle.

3. Tiger - Controlling, persistent, manipulative.

4. Panther - High level witchcraft, cause of darkness.

5. Deer - Hungry for water of the word (Ps. 42), "dear" word play, alluring eyes – could be Jezebel spirit.

6. Snake – Serpent, devourer, long tale, lies, biting mouth, puts you in confusion, or it could be Moses' righteous staff that turned into a snake to devour the unrighteous snakes.

7. Alligator - Someone in authority with lots of power and influence, Big mouth, attacks people covertly, death role, tale is bigger than a snake's tale (lies).

8. Bear - Bad temper, ferocious, bear market, Russia, evil men, anger and bitterness focused on past entanglement.

9. Dragon - High level demonic attack, Satan, evil spirit, antichrist forces, powerful influential person.

INSECTS SYMBOLS

1. Spider - Occult, spins web of deception, gossip (Isa. 59:5).

2. Ant - Industrious, team worker, can be positive.

3. Mosquito - Blood sucker, infirmed spirit, carries disease, witchcraft spirit (discerned like mosquito sound).

4. Wasp - How many? One – witchcraft, a swarm – high level attack of witchcraft.

5. Bee – Can be positive or negative. Honey bees cross pollinate – cross pollinate with different fragrances of the Lord to bring fruit, or sting.

6. Fly - Represents lies from the enemy, Satan is Lord of the Flies.

7. Butterfly - Someone going through transformation, in cocoon - dark night of the soul; beautiful but delicate.

Chapter 17

COLORS

By the dream context, decide whether the object is positive or negative; then choose the positive or negative definition of the color accordingly.

1. White - (+) Purity, holy, spirit of the Lord (Rev. 6:2) / (-) Religious spirit

2. Black - (+) Formal / (-) Sin, death, famine (Lam. 4:8, Rev. 6:5, Jer. 8:21)

3. Red - (+) Wisdom, anointing, blood of Jesus, power / (-) Anger, war (Isa. 1:18; Lev. 14: 52; Josh. 2:18, 21; Rev. 6:4 & 12,3; 2 Kings 3:22)

4. Blue - (+) Revelation, communion, Holy Spirit, heaven (Num. 15:38) / (-) Depression, anxiety, sorrow

5. Green - (+) Prosperity, growth, healing / (-) Envy, jealously

6. Purple - (+) Kingship, royalty (John 19:2; Judg. 8:26) / (-) False authority

7. Gold, amber - (+) Holy, glory, purity (Ezek. 1:4 & 8:2) / (-) Idolatry, defilement

8. Yellow - (+) Hope, gift of God,/ (-) Fear, coward, pride

9. Orange - (+) Perseverance / (-) Stubbornness, strong willed

10. Brown – (+) Compassion, humility / (-) Humanism

11. Silver - (+) Redemption / (-) Slavery, legalism, domination

Chapter 18

PEOPLE

ASK QUESTIONS ABOUT THE PEOPLE IN YOUR DREAMS

1. Who is this person in relation to you?

2. What is his/her name? What does the name mean?

3. Is this person in authority over you?

4. Are you in authority over this person?

5. What does he/represent to you?

6. How would you describe this person?

7. What characteristics/issues does the person have?

8. What kind of feeling or emotion do you have for him/her?

9. What type of relationship do you have or desire with person?

10. Is she/he behaving differently than in real life?

11. Does he/she have a supernatural countenance or glow?

12. Faceless Person - (+) Angel, messenger of God, Holy Spirit / (-) Demon

A man/woman of God in your life could represent a message from God being delivered. If an untrustworthy person from your past, it could indicate a coming situation that should not be trusted.

PEOPLE SYMBOLS

1. **Mother - Church, Holy Spirit, nurturer, or literally, mother**

2. **Father - God, wisdom, provider, or literally father**

3. **Brother - Jesus, the brethren, or your brother**

4. **Sister - Sister in Christ, sister**

5. **Friend - Jesus or friend**

6. **Pastor - Spiritual care giver or pastor**

7. **Boss - Authority, CEO, could be God**

8. **Famous person - What person represents to you; call to intercede for that person, or event.**

9. **Baby - New beginning/chapter in life; depends on you for care.**

10. **Child - Innocence, spiritual fruit, younger generation**

11. **Old person - Wisdom, holy spirit, old man = carnal natural**

12. **Faceless person - (+) Angel, messenger of god, holy spirit / (-) Demon**

VEHICLES

Vehicles represent your vocation or ministry. The vehicle that appears in your dream represents your current level of impact, and ability, or it is revealing your future ministry potential.

Ask why this vehicle and not that vehicle? Dreams reveal the truth of where you are in your relationship with the Lord.

Take notice where you are sitting in the vehicle. Are you in the driver's seat, passenger's seat, or back seat of the vehicle? Where you are sitting indicates whether you, someone, or something else is in control of your life. In the driver's seat, you are in control. In the back seat, you're allowing others to control you.

QUESTIONS TO ASK

1. **How many people can travel in this vehicle?**

2. **How fast does this vehicle travel?**

3. **Does the vehicle go on land and/or sea?**

4. **Does the vehicle fly?**

5. **Are you or someone else in control or driving the vehicle?**

6 **Is the vehicle currently used today, in the past or in the future?**

7. **How is the vehicle powered?**

VEHICLE SYMBOLS

1. **Skates - Individual ministry powered by person, requires balance, child's toy**

2. **Bicycle - One person ministry, unless a tandem**

3. **Pogo Stick - Up and down efforts, little progress**

4. **Car - Personal ministry, vocation**

5. **Truck - Ministry that will carry supplies to others**

6. **Van - Small home group, ministry**

7. **Semi-truck - Partial load of blessings coming to you**

8. **Horse - Power individual ministry**

9. **Train - Places of training, glory train, move of God, powerful**

10. **Motorcycle - Personal quick moving ministry or rebellion, pride**

11. **Ship - Ministry with large spiritual influence, mission minded**

12. **Helicopter - Small mobile ministry able to go into the heavenly realm, warfare ministry.**

13. **Airplane – Larger ministry soaring in spiritual or heavenly places**

14. **Bus - Church, group ministry, or business with great influence**

Chapter 20

NUMBERS

Numbers can be very important in a dream, and can unlock the dream's interpretation. The first source to use would be your Bible. Many numbers have a Biblical significance, and some of the Biblical meanings are as follows. Other sources include the dictionary and prophetic dictionary.

In a longer number with two or more digits, ask the Lord, if this number pertains to a chapter and verse in the Bible. For example, I had a dream where I was paying the dry cleaning bill of $48.13 for a ministry leader, and that this would be a monthly charge on my credit card. I knew the number was significant, so I asked the Lord, about the number. I heard, "Go back to the beginning." So, I went to Genesis and in Gen. 48:13, there was an obscure verse about Manasseh and Ephraim, Joseph's sons. I sent the dream to the ministry leader, and asked if it meant anything. He was very excited, for it was confirmation to him of what God was teaching him about the blessings of Manasseh and Ephraim.

Another method of interpreting a number with several digits would be to add the numbers of the digits up. For example, last night, I had a dream that a hotel room cost $219.00. I added the numbers up and the total is (12) which is the number for apostolic and government.

1. **One – God, eternal, unity, beginning**

2. **Two – Separation, division, multiplication, double**

3. **Three – Trinity, fullness, complete**

4. **Four – God's creative works, seasons, directions**

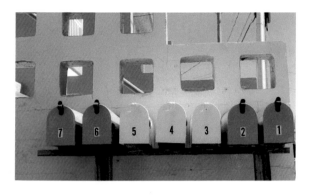

5. Five – Grace, favor, redemption

6. Six – Man's number, weakness of man, humanity, incomplete

7. Seven – God's number, completeness, perfection, fullness

8. Eight – New beginnings, new birth, teacher

9. Nine – Judgment, evangelist

10. Ten – Law, trial, testing (10 commandments, 10 plagues), wilderness, pastor

11. Eleven – Transition, prophet, prophetic intercession

12. Twelve – Government, apostle, tribes

13. Thirteen - (+) Holy, the bonding of many into one as in 12 + 1 / (-) Rebellion, corruption

14. Fourteen - Double anointing, deliverance, Passover

15. Fifteen – Mercy, reprieve, rest

25. Twenty five – Begin ministry training, forgiveness of sin

30. Thirty – Begin ministry, consecration, mourning,

40. Forty – Trials, testing, generational and completed rule.

50. Fifty – Jubilee, celebration, deliverance, freedom, debt cancelation

111. One Hundred Eleven - My beloved son

120. One Hundred Twenty - Beginning of life in the Spirit

153. One Hundred Fifty Three - Harvest, revival, evangelism, kingdom multiplication

ABOUT THE AUTHOR

 **Dale Shannon,** a Christian Life Purpose Coach, directs Fulfill Your Dream ministry created to empower and equip individuals to discover and fulfill their God given dreams, life purposes and desired outcomes. Her passion is releasing people into fullness to overcome both obstacles and limiting beliefs, and through the renewing of their minds in Christ (Romans 12:2), transform the way they perceive, think, speak, and act. Dale and her husband Doug, have two children and five grandchildren.

Made in the USA
Columbia, SC
15 October 2018